JOURNEY TO THE CENTRE

Five Point Press
ISBN: 978-1477593332

Cover image by Eileen Paul Millard; *Mind Light (detail)*
Book design by Heather Shaw

Journey to the Centre

Poems by Ann Bardens-McClellan
Art by Eileen Paul Millard

For Sarah,
dear Crystal Lake friend.
Peace, Light, and Love,
Ann

Five Point Press
2012

For our husbands, Tom McClellan and Ron Millard,
whose patience and support carried us through our journey.

CONTENTS

INTRODUCTION

WHEN I MARRIED AT 20 and had five babies in ten years, poetry was hiding in me, but it took going to graduate school much later to bring it out. In my first class at the University of Nebraska-Lincoln, a Chaucer seminar, I wrote my first poem. Something about the challenge of Chaucer, the encouragement of my professor, Paul Olson, and the death of my mother triggered a poem. Once I started, I couldn't stop and began to publish and win awards.

While getting my degrees I taught composition full-time and upon graduation took a job as course director in the composition program at the University of California-Irvine. I came to my beloved Michigan as an English professor at Central Michigan University. I taught many classes, including creative writing, establishing myself as a poet. One summer in Frankfort, I read my poems at an art opening for Eileen Millard, and we started working together.

After Canoe Press published our book of poetry and art, *Stone and Water,* Eileen and I began collaborating on a new manuscript. I earned a sabbatical from CMU and moved to Frankfort for the winter. It was a magical year. I wrote every day surrounded by Eileen's stunning artworks. She had been creating mandalas from hand-made paper, which inspired me to delve deeply into symbols and myth. Out of this yeasty ferment came *Journey to the Centre*.

I returned to teaching at CMU and Eileen began teaching art in the elementary school. We both became absorbed in teaching, although I plugged along writing poems and matching them up with the paintings Eileen had already done. Finally able to retire, I began my unexpected journey through cancer, multiple surgeries, and loss, still pouring my heart into writing poems. Last year Eileen retired and, at last, we could put the finishing touches on our manuscript. How lovely to be joining hands and voices again!

We are pleased and proud to present our work to you. We hope you read it as if you were visiting an art gallery, slowly savoring all the moods and colors of the journey

Ann Bardens-McClellan
anniethebard.com

FORTY YEARS AGO I WAS AN ART STUDENT. I earned a BFA from The University of Michigan and an MA, Art Education from Eastern Michigan University.

Thirty years ago I was a working artist, experimenting with water color, collage, drawing, papermaking and mixed media. Working from the inside out, my subjects often fell into series exploring faces and figures, nature patterns, organic geometries, spirals, ovals and circles. Working from the outside in, the works were powered by my studies in philosophy, spirituality, alchemy and religion. Seeking, always seeking...

Twenty years ago, I was planning a show when Ann and I met through a mutual friend who saw similarities in our work. Ann read at my opening reception and shortly after, we began collaborating on a book of poetry and art. Our work gelled instantly. Within the year we had published our first book *Stone and Water*. Together we created "Words and Color" workshops that we taught at art centers and colleges. We also put together a multimedia presentation of words, images, and music which we took on the road to audiences at libraries and colleges.

After several years, my artwork said to me, "You've painted your way IN, now it's time to come OUT". When news of a job teaching art to elementary students in first through sixth grade at a school near my home came to me, I jumped at the chance. For seventeen years I loved my job and the children I served.

While I was teaching, Ann was writing, editing, and sharing her knowledge of writing with the world around her. We both anticipated the time when we would be able to work together again. One year ago, I retired from teaching at my neighborhood public school and took on a volunteer job imagining, facilitating and hanging art shows at my hometown's new Art Center. I am now reinventing myself and my art.

This year Ann and I have been able to get together to craft another book of words and images. Between poetry being a language full of imagery and images being worth a thousand words, we think we've said it all. It has been a great experience to work with Ann again. We just click. Each of our work seems to support and extend the meaning of the other's. It's more like a symphony than a collaboration.

Two artists joined at the heart, soul and spirit. May readers connect with our offerings in personally meaningful ways.

Eileen Paul Millard

Journey to the Centre

THE CENTRE

In a vast white landscape
infinity cannot be written
silence is an ally
longing
leads to madness.
Lost
in absolute space
caught in winter white
I learn to break
the code.
My stolen tongue
taps out secret signals
crackling
on contact with brittle air.

THE LOST STONES OF O'NEILL
Lines for a pioneer woman

1

Maud, you were such a pretty baby,
the one with your grampa's Irish
red hair, translucent skin.

The night I lost you
your skin was blue
and underneath your tiny fingernails
purple bloomed like lilac buds.

2

Thomas, you were the quiet one
quiet even in my womb
never kicking me
never declaring your presence.
How quiet your birth. Visitors said, "You'd
never know there's a baby in the house."

When you stopped breathing
my sigh filled the house
with all the noise you never made.

3

Charles, I never could keep up with you.
You were in such a hurry to be born
I had to stop turning the wringer and lie down
I had to leave lumps in the gravy and lie down
I had to forget the dust on Aunt Emma's lamp and lie down.
My labor with you lasted so many months
I could have had ten babies . . . and
you started squalling before you left the birth canal.

We laughed, though, how we laughed.
You were the devil himself,
sneaking up, untying my apron strings
when my hands were floured and plunged into the dough.
Yes, the devil himself,
running through the house chased by Daisy
trying to whip you with her snipped pigtail.

When you came home from swimming
in the forbidden pond and
I sent you to bed without your supper,
my heart burned like the fever that finally
consumed you.

Even now my hands burn
when I remember
nights of laying cold clothes on your forehead
while the unquenchable spirit in you
dried up and died of thirst.

4
I never knew you, Walter,
crying in your cradle,
a shadow in the light of Charles.
Your cold lips refused my breast,
and when the fever took you too
it was as if you had never lived at all.

5
Grampa Frank,
you tough old coot,
you waited . . . and waited . . .
lying like a gravestone in your deathbed for six years
until they had all gone ahead of you.
What were you waiting for, old mule—
a parade of lost angels to beat the drum
for you into a heaven your Irish whiskey
and Texas tarts destroyed years and years ago?

JANEY WRITES POEMS TO HER BODY

1. Her Hair

Born with no hair, blonde
peach fuzz began to sprout on her skull,
then—a miracle—grew curly
like wild grapevines out of control.
Homely, cross-eyed Janey
with her stick legs and pasted-on
smile grew hair luxuriant
as the lilac bush outside her window.
One day, Mother lost, Father cross,
beloved Auntie takes her to live
with Grampa in the big house.
Brushing her hair, tangles
bringing tears, tenderhearted
Auntie cuts Janey's curls
one by one. *Now it won't hurt* (cutting
her glory). *Now you won't cry
and bother Grampa* (cutting her heart).
Now you'll look like Shirley Temple
(cutting her eyes).

2. Her Eyes

Her eyes go
their separate
ways, one seeing
the ceiling
of sky, the rim
of ocean, the pit inside earth,
the other peering
into the blood
of veins, the cells
of skin, the whorls
of fingerprints. Never do her eyes
see whole.

Peak Experience

3. Her Breasts

When her baby breasts began to bud
they were so tender she could not
sleep on her stomach, could not
bear clothes brushing them, could
not forget the painful blooming
beneath her shirt. Glenna in the
school yard bumped her, laughing.
Jerry hollered: *Can I see?* The pain
rose to her cheeks—to run, to hide,
to kill. No one told her how much
it would hurt to root and flower.

4. Her Ears

Tiny labyrinths,
shellike chambers
spin her round
and round, echoes
vibrating
inside her brain.
Memories hammer
her heart, truth
trapped in a maze
of false passages.

5. Her Voice

She hears her voice
caged starting to mumble,
growl. Words choked back,
swallowed, drowned, struggle
for breath, begin to erupt . . .

JANEY GETS LOCKED IN THE BOHEMIAN CEMETERY FOR THE NIGHT
for Bill Kloefkorn

You know the place,
way at the top of one of Omaha's sudden
hills. You know,
right off of Center Street, where
the sign at the gate says NO ARTIFICIAL FLOWERS
ON THE GRAVES BETWEEN APRIL I AND NOVEMBER I and
every other grave has artificial flowers and
it's only October 7. You know
how they lock the gate at midnight, so the spooks
won't escape, I suppose. Well, anyway, there she is
wandering around the graves like some lost
ghost, looking for her home--or maybe
just one too many
Bohemian beers at Lorna's Fan Tan Club
below.

She's spooky, all right,
always strolling
through graveyards, pencil and paper in her hand. What
is she really looking for, I wonder. Well, makes no
difference—that particular October
night she stays too
long and someone locks
the gate before she finishes
looking,
and so she walks all night
among the Sedlaceks and Lavickas, feeling
at home
enough by dawn to lie down and sleep beside
McCormic Mildred and McCormic James TOGETHER FOREVER
while the sun rises purple over
Woodman Tower rising
above real trees.

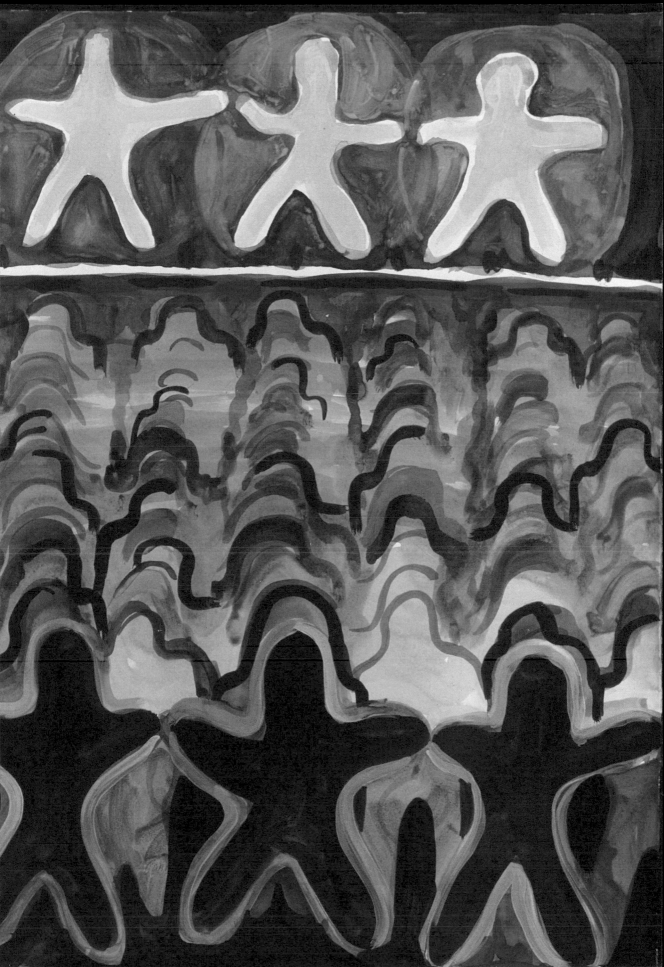

Blue Hole

HOLDING THE ANGEL

1.

Mother stands at the top
of the stairs, legs wobbling.
Her child lies in the doorway
dreaming of stairs leading
to heaven where flesh and bones
will not matter. She sits up
as her mother takes
a shaky step.

She runs, knowing her mother
will fall. No one can stop her.
Tall thin bag of bones tumbles down,
her head cracking on the step.
Her body sprawls, scarecrow
without stuffing.

2.

Each night I reach out
to catch her. Last night
I cradled her in my arms.
Tonight I am too small, too
weak to hold her. We tumble
together, arms and legs
entwined, her head broken
beneath mine.

Bandaged in white, broken
limbs lifted by pulleys
like angel wings, Mother
flies up from her hospital
bed, over rooftops, escaping
the tomb of her skin.

I am caught in rays
from the skylight,
frozen into a still life.
I see myself dressed in bunny
pajamas with ears and feet,
my arms reaching toward
an empty staircase.

ANGEL OF LIGHT

1.

We build a chair for an angel
to come and sit. She spreads
her wings over wooden arms,
leans back until her halo touches the top
rung. A chair like a ladder leads
her to heaven where she'll fly.

Her face is so soft I can barely
see her features—her isinglass
lips, her cotton ball nose. Her eyes,
though, her eyes blaze with light.
Light she rises, light she pierces,
light her nature. She sits in her
chair, casting light over our gloom.

2.

Alive in the blind dark
I call out to my angel.
I yearn for the light,
light to read, light
to learn, light to see
my way to spirit, to truth.

3.

White light opens the pages
of the book of life, blazing
with words: our hearts can
heal, our eyes can see. An
Arab is my brother, a Rabbi
is my sister. We defuse bombs
and break them down for fertilizer,
turn war games into Monopoly. Fists
soften into massaging hands.
From unadulterated soil.
we offer each other food.

BLACK ROBES

The sun's red balloon rises full
of air. Dad sits in the Warren
County Courthouse presiding over
a rape trial. When he pounds
the gavel, the balloon pops
and it's so dark I have to smell
my way out. I step outside and fall
into a pool of water sinking
almost to my chin.

Dad stands on the sidewalk in
his black robes and reaches down
to pull me out. "Janey, you're
hopeless. What am I going to do
with you?" I pull him in and say,
"Me gusta . . . me falta . . ." His robes
are wet shiny wings that lift
him so high I know I will never see
him again. Tears fall
into my laughing mouth.

Redwinged blackbirds hover over
the pool, chirping *bad girl,*
bad girl. I cry: *Get me out*
of here. Just as I am ready
to give up and drown, the water
turns warm and I float like
a balloon. I pull myself out
and stand on good firm ground.

Next Time

HAIR CUT

You tried to tame my hair
like you did my life, pouring
ashes on my fire, pinching
out the wick of my spirit.
My hair was easy, thinning,
cutting (you loved sharp
things). But deep within
a tiny spark kept smoldering.

I huddled inside the skin
prison you fashioned, no knife
to cut my way out, no match
to light the path. Mute
in the dark I gnawed the bone
of loneliness. When I looked
out, your stained eyes
stabbed me rigid.

After I smiled my way
through bruises inside and out,
ears ringing with secrets, my spirit
flared into a conflagration
nearly consuming me. It raged
until I was spent and ached
for my lake's blissful depths.

Now my body's roots
penetrate earth's core,
balancing me. My sweetheart
and I dance dark nights into light.
Pain dissolves into the poetry
of wet kisses and strong arms.
My hair flames up whenever
it wants, afire with love.

Earth Spirit

DEVIL'S FOOD

Our old house, ancient Victorian
monster, rambled over wooden box
rooms. Kitchen fridge, stove,
sink stood apart, food stored
in a pantry out of sight. Alone
Mom nipped sherry while cooking
veggies to mush and burning meat.

Sometimes Mom got out the beater
and created wonderful all-day cakes,
angel food for Sister, devil's food
with real fudge frosting for me.
On Sunday our house smelled of chicken
roasting for dinner, hot chocolate
and cinnamon toast for supper.

In our formal dining room, we sat
in walnut wiggle-proof chairs
surrounded by mahogany paneled walls,
Mirrored sideboard holding crystal
goblets reflected dark faces. Dad
talked about his day in court.
Mom sat. Sister talked about
her day in school. I sat.

Devils hid in our basement, monsters
in our closets. I never opened doors,
and walked up the stairs backwards.
Even during steamy summers I pulled
the covers over my head and held
them there as Dad's voice taunted:
*The boogeyman will get you
if you don't watch out.*

NAMING MY DAUGHTER

after Patricia Fargnoli

The one who came before she was due.
The one who tore me in my joy. The one
whose head was perfect, no marks, no dents,
no hair. She who came while the doctor
was making love to his wife. New one
with eyes squinting like a kitten's
in the glare. The first one to sail down
my river, exploring it for the sister
and three brothers who came after.

She who walked among the flowers, saying
her first word: *pretty*. She who darted
inside and out chasing butterflies. She
who discovered my sewing scissors, cutting
her hair and my best drapes. Happy one
when her fingers found piano keys. Daughter
who was a target for her father's wrath
and grown men's leers. Daughter whose
mother read Tolstoy and named her
Catherine. Daughter who stands alone
shining in her own light.

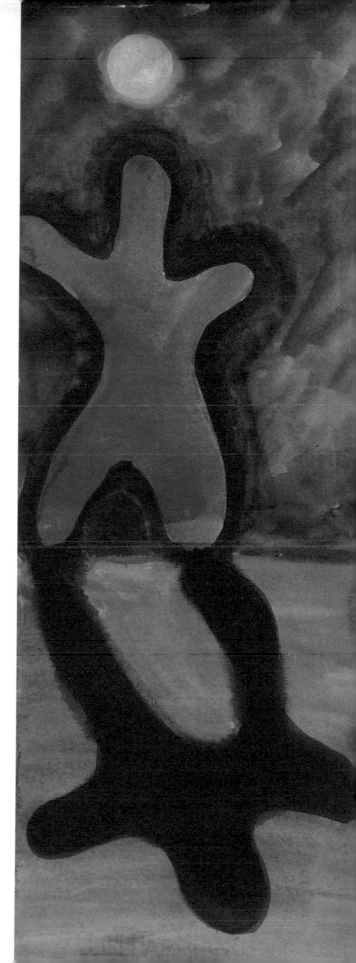

Moon Shadow

BREAKING THE LAMP, SPILLING THE BERRIES

Mom is dying, and all Dad says
to me is *Clean the house*.
When I swing the monster
vacuum around the tilt-top table,
her precious antique lamp crashes
to the floor. I watch pieces
of my mother's life shatter.

Dad's turn comes. We don't talk,
we never talk. In our final hug
his eyes grab mine, a look that breaks
open the silence. Sister says:
*I hope you didn't let Dad see
you cry*. But what do I care?
I know his secret.

Auntie Mike, who took care
of us when Mom was sick, slides
down her chair of pain to blessed
oblivion. I lay her to rest, the last
of Mom's beautiful, damaged family,
the only one to show me affection.

Today I stumble and spill a box
of blueberries, and when they hit
the floor, I see again those shards
of glass, those final looks. Dots
of blue blur through my tears.
Memories, broken by time,
burst free.

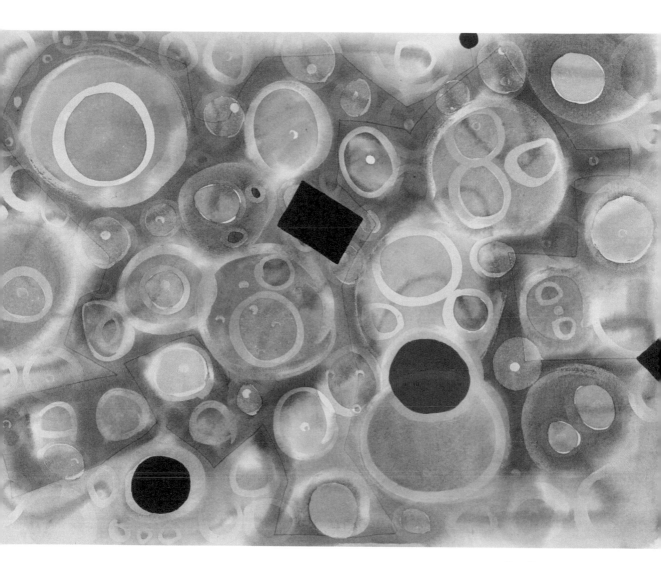

Start Here

CHANGING PLACES

1.

I dream carbon-monoxide,
razors, pills, starvation.
In the end I choose a gun,
blood and brains decorating
my white bedroom.

2.

My friend tells me
he plans to die. He wants
me to comfort him, to talk
him out of it.
I like dying
but he wants to live.

With a *What's up?*
he comes to my white
house covered in flowers.
We talk, but I know
what he really
wants. I take him
to my white bedroom
polka-dotted in red.
I've always loved you,
he says, *but how you scare
me!* I seal his lips
with mine, take
his head between
my breasts.

He succumbs.
I come alive.

Changing Faces

STEPPING STONES
for Eileen

1.
Endless flow of tides joins moon,
sun, planets. Elliptical lines
sing a silent hymn. Ocean, pure
source of life, made music
before we were born, sounds
remaining long after we are gone.
Spring tide, highest rise and fall,
comes at new moon, a swelling rush
of energy, rhythm and pitch
in perfect harmony.

2.
Mystery of our meeting
floods me with light. I enter
a landscape where water always
washes clean, rocks never fall,
and sky remains blue. Ocean waves
pound rock walls, opening them
to sacred grace. Strange mythic
being enters me, my heart
stretches, my soul shifts.
The gauze falls from my eyes.

3.
A radiant Planet guides
us as we climb ravines
of water, peaks undulating
beneath our feet. Balancing,
grasping ropes of waves, we sluice
through blind blue and green
until at last we stand
on visible white light.

4.
Our boat sails the harbor
with ease, waves lifting
us over choppy seas
like soaring on iridescent
wings. Surging through orange
boulders we reach black
headlands, and now our boat,
once so big, becomes a tiny cork
bobbing in a vast sea.

5.
Dolphins, we swim
with the stars, hearts
beating cosmic
rhythm, blood pulsing
energy of the universe.
Binding curve of space holds
us as we dance a ballet
in its airless infinity. Earth
orphans, our salvation lies
in stars and space.

Stepping Stones

Ozone Hole

BLUE STORY

after Isaak Dineson
and for Tom

You, storyteller, say
the world is two halves
of one great whole. When
you find the half matching
yours, the world becomes blue
perfection.

In the distance I hear
bells chime, striking my heart.
Blue notes weave a tapestry
of rhythms. Violet
cries dry my bones.

Swan arches her neck,
skims across blue water,
settles, then glides away.
Cornflowers dance over
russet meadow, releasing
golden seeds.

Blue light signals
that you come close.
I hold my breath, waiting
for your half to join mine
Azure sphere, broken
in two, connects,
grows whole,
blue true.

CALIFORNIA ROSE
for Tom

1.

We live inside
the curling
wave, our meditation
the held breath
before it crashes.
When I breathe
your kiss
our waves break
with one voice.

2.

To pick the rose
you must brave the thorns,
risking blood.

To find the gold
you must uncover veins
in common feldspar.

To fly with angels
you must first gallop
with your beast.

3.

Fresh-squeezed orange
juice, full of froth. radiates
light. Burgundy apples shine
amid a deep green nest of avocados.
Soft pewter reflects rose
candles. Crimson plates offer
up golden french toast, silvered
with sugar. We eat breakfast
in our own Monet.

4.

Watching the saffron
sky, I think of our colors,
once separate, blending
in a palette of amber sand,
washed by water, then merging
as vivid rose penetrates
yielding sky.

ihurt

Dedicated to Mike

it's cloudy today   too
        cloudy   i'm in here
    somewhere   i know
            because my head
                                hurts

    sky looks   like rain
        maybe   a storm of eyes
        but i can't find
            me

before my head broke   i could
    remember things
            made A's in math
    had a girlfriend   her name
                well let's see
        something sweet   maybe
            Candy   maybe
            not

i felt clean inside   now
            everything's
        fuzzy   dirty   i need
            to clean
    my glasses   what's that
            cleaner called

today
    the sky is gray
            metal
                in my head
    yesterday
            did the sun
                    shine

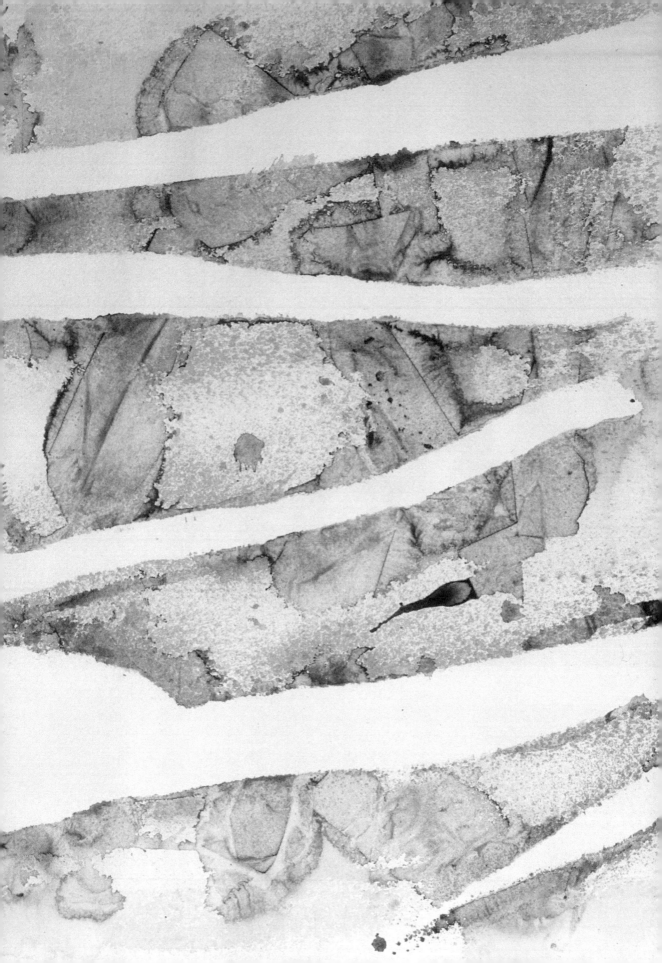

Out of the Past

THE WRONG TRAIN

The conductor points.
We wait in line.
Children cry.
A train takes off—
not the right one anyway,
We run to the next station.
A truck cuts us off.
Will we ever get home?

Lost amid nowhere trains
we drag our baggage.

Pot's on the stove.
Guests are waiting.
Table's set with Grandma's
best silver
on lace tablecloth.
Mirrors shine,
wood's polished.
Where is the hostess?

Lost amid nowhere trains
dragging her baggage.

KATHY, KATHY

Doctors cut out Kathy's breasts to save
her life. Kathy's shunt protects chemo
needles from daughter Brynna's too-tight hugs.
In their kitchen I cut veggies from the farm,
making stir-fries, soups, stews. Damocles
sword hanging over us, we eat and laugh,
Kathy's wit sharp as ever.

Steve cuts off his ponytail, shaves
his scalp to match his life-love's
head. Steve's hair makes a wig
for another sufferer. Kathy's hair
falls to the angels. Two bald heads
I caress with love.

When Kathy's breath begins to labor,
to gasp, I crawl into bed with her.
I hold her, feel her heart slow,
her breath settle. I pull her close,
crooning *It's all right.*
You can go.

Brynna cuts out paper dolls, dresses
them in full skirts, snaky red scarves.
On the school stage amid cut out sets,
she sings Gretel's song, *When at night
I go to sleep . . .* Make-believe
forest hides the truth.

Time to go, to leave the sharp-edged
mountains, snowcapped peaks fading
away. I think of Kathy, the times
we skipped stones in that deep
blue lake called Michigan
she loved so much.

Our boat's keel cuts the lake water
like a knife through human tissue.
We scatter Kathy's ashes into
the bubbling white wake. The lake
smooths out and heals itself,
blue flat calm.

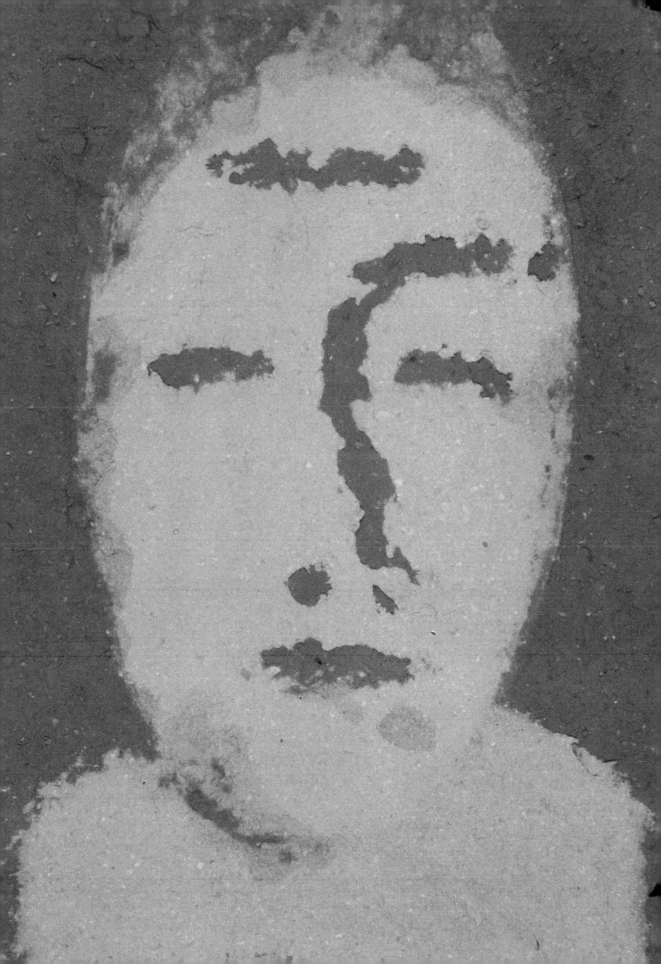

Lip Service

LOST DIALOGUE
after Elsa Tío

In your silence I feel
your first word as an animal
senses a stranger. The moon runs
searching for us in the endless
study of doves and tigers,
in the signs of serpents,
in the hidden reflections
of swamps. I am the lost dialogue
of distance and horizon.

In the spell of a forest night
I wait for you to read with me
what the branches say. I want
to fall into space like a mystery,
fall into your body like a river,
and fall into your spirit
like a nightingale in mist.
I long to be a book you read
as blind men read.

ANOTHER GRIMM TALE
for Michael Jackson

We all remember Cindy's
stepsisters cutting off the heels
and toes of their large, flat feet
to make them fit an alluring glass
slipper. What is their story?
Painting their faces, torturing
their hair, carving their flesh
to suit the kingdom's demands.

And what of the wicked
stepmother, peering into the mirror,
fearing the lines and graying
hair that tell her she's no longer
fairest of them all? Her story?
Ordering her rival taken
into the woods and killed,
her heart cut out
and kept as trophy.

Then comes the gingerbread
witch, smelling the succulent
children abandoned by their parents,
luring them into her tasty house,
fattening up the wee ones, pinching
and prodding them in an ecstasy
of hunger, salivating
for the taste
of their flesh.

And don't forget the big,
bad wolf, following the tiny
girl in her blood-red cloak
as she skips along, wanting
her and knowing he can have her
and her grandmother too. What is
his story? Donning disguises
to beguile her, pretending
to be her protector, then
revealing himself too late
as the lover who devours.

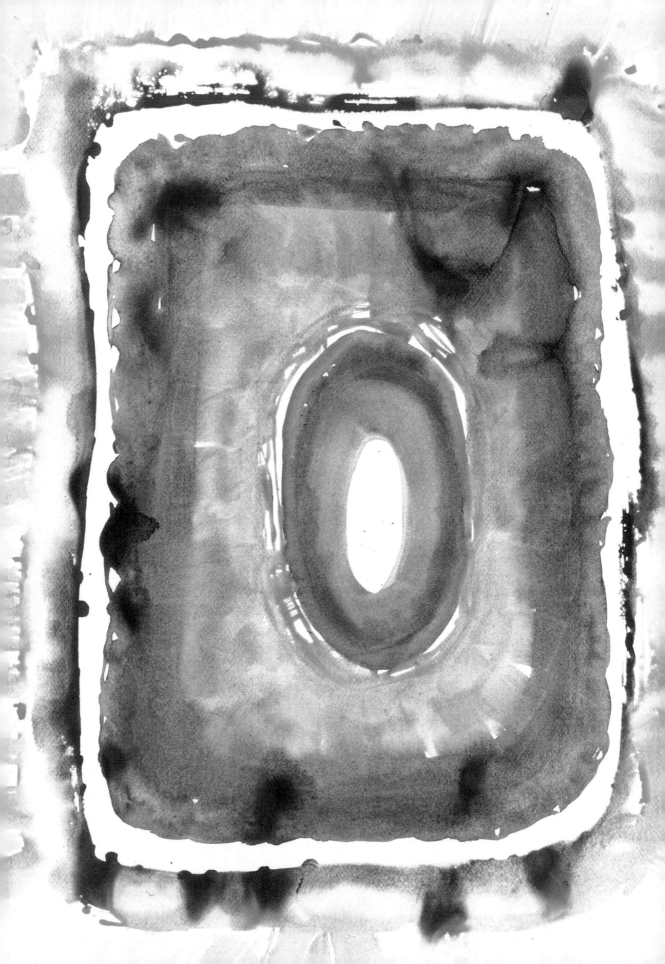

DEMETER'S LAMENT

Persephone, my beloved child, is lost to me.
I search the world for her in my chariot pulled
by winged snakes. The all-seeing, all-hearing
God of the Sun reveals that Hades has taken
her to his Underworld where she is his Queen.
I think of how Hades ravished her and I want
to kill him, kill him. But I lack the power.

I cry in rage and run from Mt. Olympus. In my grief
nothing can be born, nothing grows. Zeus relents,
and my dear daughter is sent to me for the seasons
of planting and harvesting. Embracing her again
and again, I celebrate with spring blossoms,
gathered grain, song and dance. I try to forget
that she must return to the Underworld.

When she leaves me again during harvest
festivals, I groan in grief and spread winter
over the earth. Dormant seeds will not bloom
again until she returns. All life withers
under relentless snow. My love plunges
underground, and like the cycle of seasons
I am forever caught in the wheel of grief and joy.

Liberty?

SONG OF PHILOMELA

Her ravished tongue
cannot tell of ravish.

When he took my tongue
     he broke my body
     he stole my soul.

How can I sing my song
     in a voice that's not my own?

I remember my tongue touching
the roof of my mouth,
how moist it felt,
how like a sponge.

When he took my tongue
     he broke my body
     he stole my soul.

How can I sing my song
     in a voice that's not my own?

I remember all the words
my tongue used to form,
how the sounds rolled
around in my mouth, deepening
in my throat, echoing
in my brain.

Tear out my tongue.
I will still speak,
through my body
     my bones
     my blood.
Words will pour out
like tears, like pus,
a wound that won't stop bleeding

Now I sing my song
     in a voice that is my own.

CARDINAL MEDITATION

She waits, hiding in green leaves.
He darts straight and true
to the feeder. Essence of brown
she trembles on her branch. He flicks
his wings proudly, his ripe redness
like Christmas against evergreens.

She lets him take all the glory.
Practicing his scales, he warbles
his way across the yard, skimming
grass like a frisbee. His flashing
wings carry him aloft. He feeds her.
She waits. He flies. She sits.

How I remember hiding in my box
of brown, waiting while my mate rode
the world, flashing his red damn feathers.
Sitting on my nest of eggs, I waited
for him to feed me, my voice drowned
out by his, my body his possession.

At last the female brings her brownness
to the feeder, taking a tentative peck.
She takes another and still another.
When she flies back to her nest,
she finds her chicks have flown.
Her redhead is still showing off.
Taking a deep breath, she stretches
her wings and, seeing how strong
they are, she soars.

Riverscape

homage to ee cummings

in mid-winter   when the world is ice
entombed apollo   god
of sunshine

hides   his   face

and tom and annie stay
home & cuddle
under a polarfleece
blanket

when they want to bury themselves in warm sand

the long
michigan winters trap
their souls
in static igloos turning
their bodies fetal   no-toes no-nose and

they
long
for
    spring
    when sap
runs like a river and
their
blood
churns

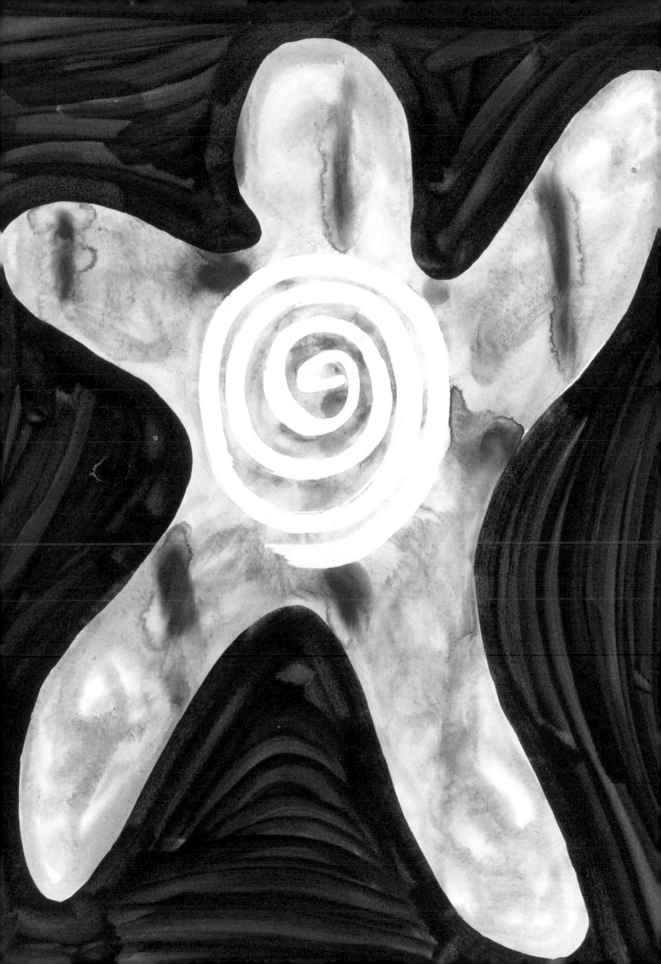

THE SPHINX OF JAZZ

Breasts of a woman, body of a lion,
wings of an eagle, she strangles
all who cannot solve her riddle.

Butterfly wings (dulcet
velvet melody) brush
my cheek like the breath
of angels telling me
where I came from where
      I am going.

My spirit knows
you, has known you
from forever.

Lightning plays tag
in ebony sky, flames arcing
      across the towers
      of our hearts
signaling syncopation.

My spirit knows.

White-hot stars spiral
up-tempo in the nebula
      dancing in air
      like notes
from a saxophone.

Breezes tease our lavendar
lake, rippling its calm surface
like a hand ruffling my hair
a voice crooning to me
of the flesh.

Oh, yes, I know.

Thistle clings to my pantlegs
riding along to our common planting
ground. We take with us
      a bit of blue hope
      savoring
the mystery of song.

THE THAWING OF LAKE WAHBEKANETTA

1.

Late winter in Michigan, ice
grows mushy around the edges
of lakes. Fishers beach
their shanties, ski runners
turned up like bobbing ducks.
Walking deliberately around
slippery snow, no paths to follow,
I see a green bench perched
on a frozen patch in the lake
inviting me to go out and sit
down, but a sign warns:
Danger: Keep Off The Ice

2.

Once lying on the surface,
A black music stand absorbed heat
from winter sun. It burned slowly
through ice, leaving a perfect crucifix.
Watching the pattern, I remember
staying up all night long ago
to make Easter coats with covered
buttons and bound button holes
for my little girls. Those navy
blue coats with yellow lining
now lie frozen in memory.

3.

In woods bordering the lake
someone with a sense of humor
has dressed the trees. They stand
tall as sentinels wearing only
underwire bras. Black on the birches,
white on the beeches—a still life
in contrast. Heavy snow has
undressed one tree, and there
it stands naked for all the
frigid world to see.

4.

Near the shore I see a toy balsa
boat embedded in ice, made from old
pieces of an airplane model
complete with stick mast
and rag sail, flapping in cold
March winds. Two acorn sailors,
caps jaunty, man the string sheet
and twig tiller, ready to
take off for the distant
spring thaw.

BURNING DOWN THE HOUSE

Today I watch your house burn,
watch the flames consume
the wood you planed and
polished, the tapestries
you wove, the loft you built
for love-dreams, and all
your dog-eared books.

How I loved your house,
the way it soared into sky,
meandered over ground and never
seemed to end, the way it fit
into the hill, taking in
fieldstones, making
them new.

In your steamy kitchen,
windows framing sweet
peas, we chopped vegetables
on marble tiles, spicy soup
simmering on the woodstove.
Toasting our feet, we read
and cuddled in your rose
afghan, surrendering
to aromas of basil and love.

But now while your house burns
I see only cold flames.

WHO WILL SAVE US?

1.

Doc rolls up his sleeves to prep
for surgery. The crowd swarms around
the room, especially the little boys.
As soon as we put them out, they come
back in. Doc tries to keep things sterile,
but I am already contaminated. Finally
he's ready, and I start undressing.

I lie on a plastic sheet at the beach.
People move in to get a better look, the men
excited. Doc puts his instruments in me
and pulls out a baby, barely formed, then puts
her back in. Do I want her? We go to ask my Tom
if he wants to try and save her, but Doc says,
With her problem, we can't save her anyway.

2.

The man is tall, handsome, flirtatious,
and I have crush on him. Along
with family and friends, I invite
him to our Labor Day outing. I ask
him to bring me a knife for the picnic
basket, but he sends my daughter instead.
Contriving to get closer to him,
I ask him to drive my car. *I lost
my glasses*, I say. We all travel
in separate cars and lose track
of each other.

Before we can get our caravan together
again, he takes one of the Arabs,
slides a piece of wood in his captive's
mouth to keep him from screaming,
and kills him. He strips himself
of his outer shell and walks like
an ordinary man into the crowd.
He thinks he's saving us.

Cosmic Beach

3.

In a huge concentration camp
we're being watched by hidden
cameras. Thousands of us just sit
there, quiet, unmoving, docile.
A Liam Neeson look-alike tumbles
out from the crowd, raising his fist.
We try to move, shuffling our feet,
but see no place to go. Our leader
leaves us.

Dark-haired women dressed
in vivid saris break free,
spill across the grass, laughing
and singing—a splash of spirit
and color like birds on a gray day.
We enjoy but do not join them. Soon
they too fly away.

Another rebel (is it Tom?) breaks out
shouting, *Save yourselves*, and this time
we join him. We're terrified, but we realize
we have to do something, or we'll sit
here under surveillance the rest
of our lives. Unsaved.

ILLUSION MASTER

I

Come on, come on, little lady,
Try your luck with the little red ball.
Three throws for a dollar.
Win the purple panda
                    with beautiful
                              pink eyes.

Come on, come on
He's so soft.
Touch him touch him
He won't bite.
Touch him, touch him
He won't hurt you.
Tell him anything you want to
Pandas don't talk back.

II

Welcome to my house of mirrors.
Step on my ramp, glide through my glittering palace.
Let me show you who you really are.

My first mirror ripples like ribbons
        bunched for a bridal bouquet.
Look and see how beautiful you are,
        hair raining pearls,
        immaculate dress enfolding
        newborn breasts pale as morning
        light falling on your pillow.

My second mirror bellies out,
        a fat glass Falstaff,
Look and see how fruitful you are.
        seed held high under your heart,
        skin singing a lullaby,
        swollen womb a resurrection.

My third mirror spins a globe in space,
    a head without a body.
Look and see how wise you are.
Streams of thought cut chasms in your face,
Balm of your voice anoints
    kneeling supplicants.
Your fervent lips,
    touching each bowed head,
    thrill passion and power.

My fourth mirror, a ghostly prism, flickers
    a tallow face, a skeleton body.
Look and see how haunting you are.
Milky eyes peer into shadows, glimpsing only mist.
Behind you lies the wreck of years,
    junkyard in a whirlwind,
    a rag doll body stripped of stuffing,
    button eyes torn loose and dangling.
Can't you see?
Can't you see?
Eyes have lost their vision.
Breath clouds up my mirror.

Move back, old crone, so someone else can
    look and see who they really are.
Step off the ramp—careful now—
    your turn is over.

. . . come on, come on, little girl
three throws for a dollar . . .

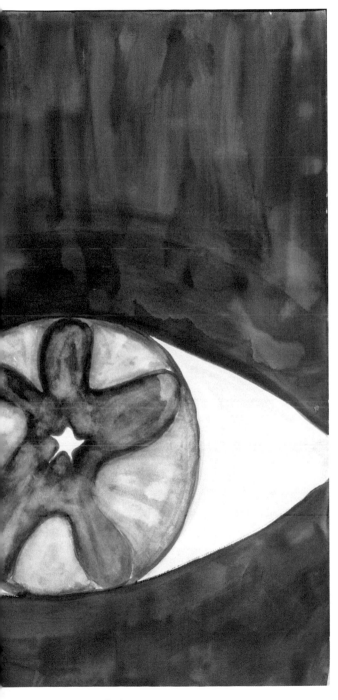

Eye I

BACKWARD CHILD

Broken,
tiny glasses mend
like magic as the baseball
flies away from her face. Blood
flows back into her nose, tears
dry. Classmates' taunting
grins grow indifferent.
Terror hides
in her false smile.

Father's hand
backs away from her bare
bottom, wet fingers poised
in midair. She stands at the door
where she has been waiting
since Mother yelled: *You just
wait 'til your father comes
home. He'll give you a spanking
you won't forget.*

Gagging stops
as Grandfather's huge limb
leaves her mouth and shrivels
to a withered branch. Her scream
reenters her mouth, dying
as she swallows it. Ogre
backs out of her bedroom
into darkness. Her mouth
tastes baby clean.

She feels
herself growing smaller
her mind shrinking. Soon
she's aware only of food
and sleep. Her fingers and toes
fascinate her. One day noises
flashing lights and pain dissolve.
Unborn, all she knows now
is sweet silence.

LULLABY

Hush, little baby,
don't say a word.

Don't cry, baby,
Grampa wants to make
you feel good, ohh baby,
feels so good. Grampa loves
you good.

Pappa's gonna buy you
a mockin' bird.

Hush, child, hush,
don't you cry, don't
you tell. If you tell
our secret your tongue will fall
right out, your gramma's ghost
will haunt you. Baby, if you ever tell,
Grampa will sneak back
and chop off
all your fingers.

If that mockin' bird
don't sing

She's so shy, won't say a word.
What's a'matter, child,
cat got your tongue?

Pappa's gonna buy you
a diamond ring.
If that diamond ring
turns brass
Pappa's gonna buy you
a lookin' glass.

TRUTH AND FICTION

after viewing the painting
by Charles Murphy

He holds her head with his long
blue and white arms. He looks
into the distance, not seeing her,
only noticing a loaf-of-bread
mailbox covered in snow.
Mail comes from so far away,
through blue trees, green air,
checkered table cloths, arriving
too late to save her. The black cloak
covers her, pulling her into darkness.
Orange flame of life fades.

He loves her. Look how tenderly
he holds her, how he shields her body
with his strong shoulders. Her face
presses into his cheek. She sobs.
He looks away, unable to bear
her pain. Orange sun circles
them diffusing color through
his veins into her heart. Her body
warms, releasing gold dots into blue air.
Gold collars on their robes fuse. The black
cloak falls away. She steps out.

THE WALL

1.

They lock us inside
the gates of their prison
hands tied behind us, mouths
taped. Our silent screams
reach upward and finding no
succor, turn inward, piercing
our own hearts.

In our cells, hands freed,
we scribble messages with fire's
charcoal on rough toilet paper.
We pretend to communicate
with each other, with our loved
ones outside.

2.

We stand at the wall
our bodies sacks
of cement, eyes blades,
mouths flint, each mind
a homemade bomb.

Searching the sky we see
a hawk circling above us.
She dips earthward, then swoops
again toward heaven. Her majestic
flight bears prayers to God,
returns grace to earth.

We poke paper doves
onto barbed wire
where they flutter
helpless in the wind.
Our captive fingers release
them one by one. Weeping
we watch them rise.

BLOOD IN THE SNOW, 1905 REBELLION
after Symphony 11 by Shastakovich

There, there they lie, butchered
bodies in the Winter Palace snow
red smearing pristine white.
In the silence we see defenseless
bodies dotting the landscape, blood
pouring like royal fountains
through their workers' clothes.

Overhead, shrieks of vultures
punctuate the silence like bullets
tearing through flesh. We watch
from a great distance, eardrums
pierced by pain, hearing only
the beating of our own hearts.
We cry unheard tears, knowing
the violence to come.

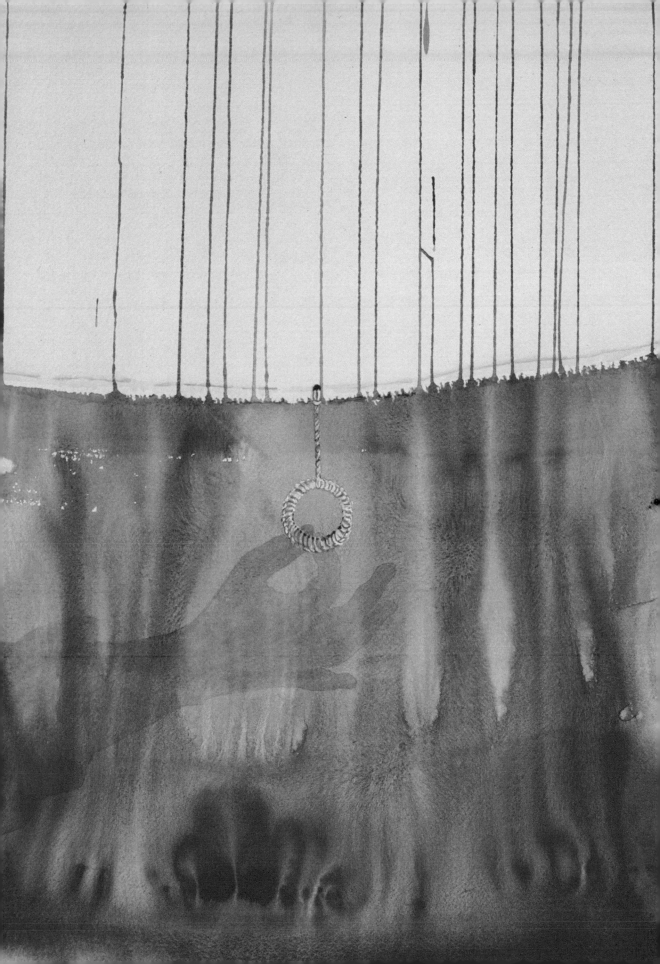

OCEAN SONGS

Blessed be the Pacific, waves peaceful
on a sunny day, ferocious in a storm.
Blessed be rocks and shells tossed
by wild surf, wet colors mingling
with buff sand. Sand dollars, so rare
today, still tell their tales of graceful
fossils. Wet-suited surfers strut
like penguins, while arthritic joggers
fold their crane-like legs.

Blessed be tidal pools, home for
crustaceans whose ancestors created
this beach. Blessed be whales spouting
in deep water as they migrate to Mexico.
How we long for warm breezes, bare
feet on hot sand, short skirts
and sandals, frozen Margaritas rimmed
in salt, briney water stinging our eyes.
We open our pores to the blessed sun.

Coral Reef

REFLECTIONS
for Tom

1.

Swinging artists, we draw and write
while listening to jazz, facing
that nightmare of the single life,
the blind date, my friend set up
with a "wonderful man." Oh
yeah, we've heard that before.

With a beatific smile, he opens
the door, and kindness floods
my heart. His date is blind
to what I see. He takes his pencil
and draws my face, making a circle
of shadow outside a circle of light.
Inside I glow, filled with chiaroscuro.

I read my poems, seeing his eyes
upon me, his face framed in light.
One poem doesn't quite work
and when I sit down beside
him I ask for a word. *Luminous*,
he says, yes, *luminous in moonlight.*

2.

Last night I dreamed you came
to me, tall as a house, slender
as a shadow, dark as daybreak.
Your sweet smile, a beam of light,
blinded me for a moment and when
I could see again, you turned
into a peppermint stick.

We run to the field to fly
our kites in the gentle breeze,
soft as your breath, strong
as your arms. You release
your kite and it soars blue
into tawny sky, its green
streamer trailing. You reach
for mine, but I let it go free

and your delicious strawberry
fingertips touch my cheek,
my lips, my breast, then sink
sweetly into me like angel light
sealing the tender membrane
of our union.

3.

I am becoming yours, a piece
of earth you sow and cultivate,
a tree you plant and water. Come
to my fields and plant yourself.
We will grow together, two trees
twining into one.

Your stained glass prism hangs
in my window, reflecting every
color on my skin. I see
that everything emerges
from the emerging self.

Our mirror leads us inside
ourselves again and again.
We slide under its transparent
surface and find the gift
of our own reflection.

ICARUS
for a hang glider pilot

You come
out of the sky, soaring
over sand, wings
laced across your back, legs
dangling like a seagull,
at home in the air.

Prisoner to earth,
I watch, body yearning
toward the sun, arms aching
to stretch and fly,
my envy palpable.

Only in dreams
do I dare sprout
wings, do I dare
let my legs dangle
over nothingness.

Awake, my earthbound
mind will not release
my body, letting it lift
like yours into the light.

Ann Takes Off

OWL AND EAGLE

for Tom

1.

Day begins with Eagle spreading
her wings, luminous in sun's full
light. She flies through thunder
and fire, powerful as Venus, swift
as Mercury. Lion of air, she devours
earthly creatures, sacrificing lower
forces to divine majesty. Thunderbolt
she is—her wings, spirit, her flight,
imagination. Her feathers, threads
shot through with fire, capture
the eye of man, transforming
him into lover. Her beating wings,
the pulsing of his heart, she lifts
him into incandescent air.

2.

Night falls, flame burns low, colors
soften into smoky sky. Spent
Eagle flies to her nest
settling her wings in peace.
Sleeping Owl awakens, his wings
unfolding from his burnished body,
blending now with shadows. His
unveiled eyes seek—as head rotates
on body—invisible prey. Magician
of night, he pulls dead sun
across a dark sea, his music full
of sonorous tones. He soars to moon's
Merlin light, his descent unleashing
terror into germinating darkness.

3.

Owl, lit by fire, bursts once more skyward,
joining Eagle, Together, balanced for flight,
they flare into divine indigo eye.

Day joins light and life, word and thought,
eternal logos. Night reveals the path
leading back to mystery of all origin.

THE LANGUAGE OF SPIDERS
after Elsa Tío

1.
When endless space whets
her appetite for swallowing
time the spider   her stitches
made of air   weaves her web
of dust and mystery
mid light
mid shadow
mid fear.
Her thread   without needle
never harmed by wind
still as silver
soft as dreams
spins the surface of silence
into tired old corners.

Always alone   she weaves
a language of ghosts
and one evening star.

2.
The spider   no longer omen
of regret   crawls across the moon
swallowing its energy. From her
body
she spins filaments of light
tracing mysterious webs
in ebony sky. From earth

we watch as she sails
like thistle-down   threads
levitating her body above us.
We wait balancing on dust
for her to drop feather-
like on our ground.

3.
Spider dreams weave
portraits in image
and word.
Makers we draw fragile strength
from our bodies creating
order from signs
spirit
memory.

4.
Madre de Dios sews
with a spindle inside
mountains of stone
weaving her thread
into the spider's web.
Together they create
the language
of stars
of grass,
a magic spiral
connecting
earth and sky.

UNLEARNING LOGIC

If A worships a snake relic and B
handles snakes to prove his faith,
then C concludes they are satanic,
but what if A says: *No way am I
only part of a syllogism. I will
be the first woman president or
secretary general of the UN.*
And C imagines himself
as much more than the conclusion
of any two premises. Sometimes
he's a cloud pulled through the sky
on a chariot of wind, losing parts
of himself to make rain or gathering
other droplets to form the huge
belly of a storm. And B,

shy B, writes poems in his closet
poems to make the world put down
its weapons. C reads these poems
and smiles, raining drops of love
on A who dances in wet grass
forgetting her labors. A,
bold A, passion rising, kisses
B, touches his eyes, his lips
with her shining fingers.
C divides letting the sun
illuminate them. They all weep
at the depth of B's poems and peace
yes   peace will come.

Hummingbird's Eye View

A MAUVE DAYDREAM

Back in my childhood home,
Mom dead, Dad gone, I lie
in my canopy bed. I'm surrounded
by blue wallpaper I chose long ago,
tiny forget-me-nots clustered
in rows. Hand-tatted bedspread
reminds me of Queen Anne's Lace
dotted across a mauve
thyme field.

Illinois summer sticks
to my forehead and I remember
steamy days canning applesauce,
its sweet-sick stench lodged
in my nose. When I drop a jar,
broken glass, sharp as Mom's voice,
cuts my foot. Blood mingles
with dust on the floor creating
a mauve painting.

Oh how I long to be
at our Michigan cottage.
Where sea scows race in lakes
bluer than the vase on my dresser.
Where wind flaps the sails
like eyelet-trimmed sheets
on washday. Storm clouds
on the horizon warn us to head
for our berth. Our ship's mast,
tall as a sentinel, salutes
the mauve sky.

WHY I LOVE TWILIGHT

Ah, I've survived another autumn day,
trees heavy with branches, summer leaves
still clinging. Sunset spreads its fiery
promise of another chance to shine.
When darkness falls I catch wisps
of words in my net.

I stand above the city watching lights
blink on, creating a necklace snaking
through the crook of shadows. The sun
with all its shouting is gone, and
rivers of darkness begin to pierce
the night, restoring me as I write.

By morning I will leaf through pages,
finding buds of the night I can keep,
discarding twisted branches. My work
ends as light begins to filter through
the soft sky. As the world awakens,
I sink into blissful sleep.

WORDS ARE MY MUSIC

I longed to play the piano,
but Mom said *No, you're too shy.*
Music was my life and secretly
I danced and sang. I saw myself
composing oratorios, ballets,
symphonies. All I could manage
to compose was myself.

I am shy no longer, but my fingers
are stiff. My legs are stiff too.
I still ski walk through the burnt
sienna leaves of fall, but I don't
boogie to "Heartbreak Hotel" or
"I've Got a Rock and Roll Heart."

An old tape plays in my head: *Scaredy- cat,*
 scaredy-cat. But I'm brave enough
now to face down death and cancer.
I still hear all the tunes I never
wrote, the melodies in my head
singing and beating time.

No one can take away my song.

AGAINST GRAVITY
for Bobbi, the potter

Brown eyes snapping
in your gentle face,
you show me your winged
sculpture in the kiln. Hands
together as if in prayer
you say: *I hope it's not*
too heavy, too thick to fire
without cracking.
I have to try.

We walk the beach,
and see the gull, wings
still spread in flight, tips
of blue feathers pointing
the way...
       once it soared,
        its body a kite ...
now neck snapped,
body crumbling in sand,
its spirit still resists death
in every broken bone.

Watching the dip and flow
of shore birds, I think
of your potter's kiln baking clay
you have formed with your mind,
with your hands. I see the sculpture
crack and you, breathing a sigh,
set your jaw, begin again ...

Reborn, the sculpture rises
like a gull skimming across water
on determined wings.

       oh that moment
       when you lift off and fly
       on your own taking breath after breath of pure air
       riding the crest of the current ...

I surrender my gravity
to your grace. Heat of your fire
transforms my voice. My words
take wing and
weightless
they fly.

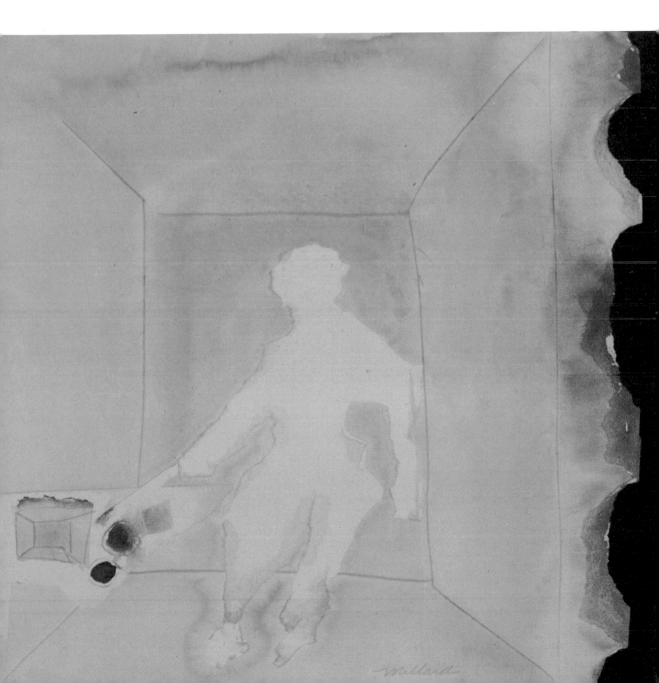

ACKNOWLEDGEMENTS / ANN BARDENS-MCCLELLAN

Awards:

'The Lost Stones of O'Neill," Award winner, judged by Etheridge Knight
"Illusion Master," Award winner, judged by Colete Inez
"Janey Gets Lost In the Bohemian Cemetery for the Night," Gwendolyn
    Brooks Poetry Award
"Truth and Fiction," Honorable Mention, Shaw Prize, *Dunes Review*
"Hair Cut," First Prize, Poet's Night Out Competition

Publications:

"The Lost Stones of O'Neill ," anthology, *All My Grandmothers Could Sing*
"Illusion Master," *Plainsongs*
"Another Grimm Tale," *The MacGuffin*
"Blue Story," *Garfield Lake Review*
"Janey Gets Locked in the Bohemian Cemetery for the Night," *Mid America
    XXV*
"Burning Down the House," *Dunes Review*
"Backward Child," anthology, *Times of Sorrow, Times of Grace*

GRATITUDE:

Paul Olson, for seeing potential in me that I didn't know was there.
Eileen Millard, my soul-sister.
My poetry group, for being kind while being tough.
Heather Shaw, for expert design.
Marcy Branski, proofreader extraordinaire.
Tom McClellan, my first and most sensitive reader.

ACKNOWLEDGEMENTS / EILEEN PAUL MILLARD

*Mind Light	Shield series/acrylic and wood on canvas	39"x 39"
Peak Experience	Star People series/watermedia on paper	22" diameter
Standing Room Only	Star People series/watercolor on paper	30"x 22"
Waiting	Conte crayon on paper	22"x 15"
Heart Light	Shield series/acrylic and wood on canvas	39"x 39"
Next Time	Political Papers series/dyed handmade paper	30"x 33"
Serious One	Faces series/dyed handmade paper	17"x 11"
Earth Spirit	Faces series/watercolor on handmade paper	18" diameter
*Moon Shadow	Star People series/watercolor	11"x 30"
Start Here	Watercolor	22"x 30"
Changing Faces	Face series/dyed handmade paper	28"x 28"
*Stepping Stones	Watercolor	30"x 22"
*Ozone Hole	Watercolor/pearlescence on handmade paper	18" diameter
Ode to Georgia	Poured watercolor series	30"x 22"
Through the Blind	Sprayed watercolor	30"x 22"
Out of the Past	Dance of Life series/watercolor	22"x 30"
Buddha Calm	Faces series/dyed handmade paper	17"x 11"
Lip Service	Circle series/watermedia on handmade paper	18" diameter
Big Head	Watercolor on tableau paper	51"x 39"
*Life Underground	Watercolor	30"x 22"
Liberty?	Face series/watercolor	18" diameter
Riverscape	Watercolor triptych	each panel 30"x 22"
Creativity	Star People series/watercolor	30"x 22"
*Sphinx	Watercolor	12"x 9"
Lion and Lamb	Watercolor	22"x 32"
*Sun Spirit	Face series/watercolor with paper pulp relief	30"x 22"
*Cosmic Breath	Watercolor	22"x 30"
Moon Spirit	Faces series/watercolor with paper pulp relief	22"x 30"
Eye I	Star People series/watercolor	30"x 22"
Empty	Watercolor	30"x 22"
Embrace	Watercolor	22"x 15"
The Wall (1 of 3 shown)	Political Paper series/dyed handmade paper	36"x 24"
Pull the Shade	Sprayed watercolor	30"x 22"
*Coral Reef	Mandala series/watercolor on handmade paper	18" diameter
Mirror Mirror	Watercolor	30"x 22"
Ann Takes Off	Acrylic on Paper	116"x 34"
Feathered Shield	Oval series/watercolor	30"x 22"
Space Web	Dyed handmade paper	27"x 30"
Running Figure	Paper assemblage with watercolor	30"x 22"
*Hummingbird's Eye View	Watercolor on handmade paper	18" diameter
The Road North	Watercolor and collage	22"x 30"
Heart Explosion	Mixed watermedia collage	30"x 22"
The Artist in Her Studio	Watercolor with collage	22"x 22"

* these works are in private collections

Most of the other original works are available (unframed) from the artist.
Contact: millards51@gmail. com or P.O. Box 427, Frankfort, MI 49635